Presented to

....

on the occasion of

....

With love from

....

Celebrating Motherhood

Lion Publishing
1705 Hubbard Avenue, Batavia, Illinois 60510, USA
ISBN 0 7459 2395 X

First edition 1993

Library of Congress Cataloging-In-Publication Data
Hathaway, Mary
    Celebrating motherhood / Mary Hathaway
    ISBN 0-7459-2395-X
    1. Motherhood—Religious aspects—Christianity.
    2. Motherhood—Biblical teaching. 3. Motherhood
    —Poetry. I. Title
    BV4529.H35 1993 92-38993
    242'.6431–dc20 CIP

Printed and bound in Malaysia

Acknowledgments
Photographs by Stephen J. Dorey: pages 42/43;
Ebenezer Pictures/David Keel: pages 36/37; The Image
Bank/Reagan Bradshaw: page 30; Lion Publishing:
pages 11, 14, 16, 17, 21, 22/23, 25, 29 , 33, 35, 38/39,
43; Nicholas Rous: pages 32/33, 40; Stockphotos/
Sandy King: page 26/Derek Smith: page 28; Tony
Stone Photolibrary–London/Fiona Alison: page 10/
Andy Cox: page 12/13/Andrew Sacks: page 31; ZEFA/
Tom Casalini: page 15/Wayne Eastep: pages 20/21/
David Hall: endpapers/M. Hamel: pages 24/25/
Michael Keller: page 12/Gary Kufner: pages 40/41/
Deborah Levinson: pages 18/19/Kelly/Mooney: pages
5 and 34/Milt/Patti Putnam: pages 16/17/ Bob
Taylor: pages 26/27/ Jeff Turnau: pages 44/45

CELEBRATING MOTHERHOOD

Mary Hathaway

A LION BOOK
Oxford · Batavia · Sydney

TO JOHN AND RICHARD,
WHO GAVE ME MY MOTHERHOOD

INTRODUCTION

In this book I have tried to share with you what being a mother means to me. I have gathered together some moments of special joy, but these always happen alongside problems and difficulties so I have tried to reflect them too. I am well aware that motherhood is a demanding business! The pieces of my writing that I have selected for this book have been written over many years and were not originally intended for publication. They are a record of the pleasures and frustrations that my children have given me.

Money on its own cannot give our children happiness. That involves the giving of time and love to children. But I have found trying to do just this one of the most worthwhile things in my life. For children who experience real love are able to pass it on, so what I am doing now can be of value to future generations.

So this is a celebration of motherhood, a statement that, in spite of the pressures, being a mother is something to be enjoyed. My children have given so much to me. Not only have they given me times of laughter and happiness but they have also helped me to build up my own personality and have enriched my life.

Mary Hathaway
February 1992

Joy and laughter

The Lord has filled my heart with gladness,
he has given me joy and laughter!

At last I am satisfied,
for I have found part of myself
I have always been looking for
in the tiny person
of my new-born child!

In the time of harvest

Creator of all things, giver of life, you watched over this child as she grew in my body through the months. Now the fruit of our creative love has been born, in the time of harvest.

Harvest—the culmination of the earth's age-old cycle, yet holding in its hands the promise of spring, an ending and a beginning. For inside the fruits yielded by the earth lie the seeds of next year's harvest. Our child is the harvest of our hearts and souls and the beginning of a new life for us, the hope of all that is to come.

Watch over the sowing of love in this young life and guide us through the early months of tenderness and care while we get used to the tremendous miracle that is our child, feeling hesitant and sometimes inadequate. Over the years as the seed takes root, help us all to grow in love and wisdom. Grant that we may see the harvest in her life. May we rejoice in the remembrance of this time when harvest and springtime came to us in the birth of our first child.

F IRSTS

First smile

From your birth
my love shone into you
and smouldered into flame.
Love was kindled in you,
lighting lamps in your
eyes—
today I saw the beginning
of all your loving
in your first smile.

First steps

So you walked between us,
you laughed and we laughed,
the three of us
in a circle of joy.

First one, then two,
oh, just a bit shaky—
would you fall?
Our eyes shone with love
and anticipation.
You did it!
Three steps on your own
for the very first time,
hugs and kisses all round!

We were amazed at such a miracle.
What a wonderful moment
sparkling with joy
when you took your first steps
walking from love into love!

Spring morning

I recall
a spring morning,
a low stone wall
and yellow alyssum in the sun,
trees full of blossom
and a mother with her baby,
just five months old,
seeing spring for the first time.

And now it is winter,
the trees are wet and bare
and the wind is cold.
The child, warmly dressed,
takes uneven steps
and laughs at the winter sun.

But I see again that morning
when the whole world
was filled with love
and held only
a mother with her baby,
trees full of blossom,
and a low stone wall
and yellow alyssum in the sun.

These quiet hours

The curtains surround
a pool of stillness
filled with gentle light
and gentle darkness
from the tall lamp
with shade of muted gold.
We sit, the two of us,
in the one time of the day
which is just for each other.

In silence I watch
the fleeting expressions
on your face, so mobile, so alert,
soaking up each detail
of the room.
Every part of you throbbing with life
yet gladly absorbing
the stillness.
Each moment like a story
never to be retold.
Neither yesterday nor tomorrow
can have these special joys.

So our love finds room
to expand in the stillness;
our knowledge of each other
grows a little more each day
in the unhurried lamplit joy
of these quiet hours.

First butterfly

On the bare earth
lies a painted flower
with quivering petals—
a butterfly, a butterfly,
the first butterfly of spring!

'Come quickly!
I want to show you,
see the wonder on your face,
I want to see you
seeing your first butterfly!'

But he wanders up the path,
he senses no urgency.
Why should he?
Life is just beginning.
He has all the time in the world.

The butterfly trembles
and is gone.
I laugh at myself
for my impatience.
For he has all his life
to find beautiful moments
and butterflies.

Jesus said . . . 'I assure you
that unless you change and
become like children you will
never enter the kingdom of
heaven.'

MATTHEW 18:3

An ordinary evening

After the evening meal
the family sat around the table
when suddenly—

'Look, there's a woodpecker,
on the old apple tree.'
'Lesser, greater, green?
Quick, Dad, where're the binoculars?'

A flash of color and pattern
so bold and bright
it seemed to me
it should be in some
tropical jungle
not in our small back yard.
Red, black and white
glowed like jewels
in the evening sun . . .

'It's lesser spotted
—isn't it close?'

As they decided,
it flew away.
And I was left
with a memory of beauty
and an evening
that had become ordinary
once again.

Love laughter

Some laughter is good
and some is bad,
but there is pure laughter,
there is joyous laughter,
when a child laughs at the morning
brilliant with sunlight,
spontaneous and free.

And there is the laughter
that spills over from a heart
that is filled to the brim with love.

This laughter is warm, gentle and kind.
It is always joyous, pure and lovely.

May you know early in your life, my child,
this best gift of love laughter.

Laughter is the sun that drives winter
from the human face.

VICTOR HUGO

Small child in spring

She stands, diminutive,
among rhododendrons
and azaleas that seem
to her so tall
they reach the sky.
Where the branches
meet above her head,
she walks in tunnels
shrouded green in mystery,
whose walls are decked
with flowers.

Red, magenta, purple,
yellow, salmon pink and
white,
with petals cool and crisp,
spotted like orchids,
their scent enfolds her
with exotic joy.
Each fallen flower
is held in reverent hands
and bathed in wonder
from her shining eyes,
then threaded into garlands
with delight.

Then she finds the path
which winds upwards
between great banks
of yellow flowers,

and, as she climbs,
their golden trumpets
fill the air with music
and angels sing of God
in rainbow colors.

Up and up until in some way
she cannot understand
she almost reaches heaven
and looks down upon
the paradise of flowers
and stands alone
in her enchanted kingdom.

The news—by a five year old

'I've got some wonderful news for you, Mom,
some wonderful news.'

'I went down the hill
and saw a ladybird

so red and shiny
with tiny black spots.
And it moved—
it was alive!
But that's not all, Mom.
The ladybird came
right on to my finger
and I watched it crawl
right across my hand!'

'And that, Mom,
is the most wonderful news
in the whole wide world!'

Miracle of nature

I am deeply grateful
when I see all new-born things
that I have a part
in life's perpetual turning,
the ceaseless round
of life, birth, death
and rebirth.

In fall the world dies
in such a glorious way
it hardly seems like death.
Even the smell of decay
is fragrant
and the ground is pungent
with wet and dying leaves.

But fall's grave
becomes the cradle
in which spring is born.
Nature is never without hope.
Winter is only her travail
before the miracle of birth.
Then come new leaves,
bluebells laugh
and ducklings swim
around their mother,
life has begun again.

And I too have carried
a child within me,
I have travailed

and passed on life.
Now I no longer
look from the wings
at this great drama.
I bow my head with thanksgiving
that I have known pain and joy,
that I too at last
have become part
of this great rhythm of life.

There is a time for everything, and a season
for every activity under heaven.

ECCLESIASTES 3:1

Gentle touch

Falling leaves,
yellow, green and
brown,
silently
covering the ground,
blanketing, healing
the scorched earth
of summer.

Gradually, quietly,
one by one,
days passing
unhurried,
healing the mind
scorched and scarred
by suffering.

Falling leaves,
passing days,
each one
a gentle touch,
restoring the ground
with compassion,
ready for rebirth.

Starting School

Tomorrow you are starting school. I have tried to prepare you, encouraging you to be independent and helping you to be happy away from us. It is a big step for you, spending a large part of each day in a new environment and to be just one child in a class of many.

You will have to sort out problems on your own and come to terms with things you do not like. You will know joy and sorrow but I will not be there to share them. You are beginning to live your own life, separately from ours. How will you cope? How will I cope?

But this I know: my prayers for you rise steadily, daily, covering every part of your life. I need never feel completely cut off from you because through them my love can always reach you wherever you are. My love and my prayers are a gentle, enfolding garment, but also a strong protective armor to surround you always.

Leave all your worries with
him, because he cares for
you.

I PETER 5:7

Don't worry about
anything, but in all your
prayers ask God for what
you need, always asking him
with a thankful heart.

PHILIPPIANS 4:6

Prayer for a sick child

Lord, my child is sick. I know there are millions of children all over the world who are victims of famine, disasters, wars and disease and they are much more needy than my child who has a home and parents and doctors to look after him. But my child is sick, Lord, and there are times when I feel inadequate watching him suffer, weary as I am with constant nursing and broken nights.

Please look upon my child. Let your love flow through me and when I fail, let your love take over. For you love each child everywhere as if they were the only child in the world. They are always covered by the smile of your love, and you suffer with them in their pain. Smile upon my child tonight, Lord, for he is also one of your little ones.

Some people brought children to Jesus for him to place his hands on them, but the disciples scolded the people. When Jesus noticed this, he was angry and said to his disciples, 'Let the children come to me, and do not stop them, because the Kingdom of God belongs to such as these. I assure you that whoever does not receive the Kingdom of God like a child will never enter it.' Then he took the children in his arms, placed his hands on each of them and blessed them.

MARK 10:13–16

Thanksgiving after illness

For eyes beginning to brighten,
for color stealing back into pale cheeks,
for the flicker of a smile,
and then the first laugh for days—

I thank you, Lord.

For tiny meals eaten at last,
for peace where there was pain and distress,
for a little child running into my arms
who hadn't the strength to sit up—

I thank you, Lord.

For the sound of happy chatter,
for the interest shown in a new book,
for lifting the shadow over our hearts
and putting sunshine in our home again—

I thank you, Lord.

Your birthday

So much has happened
in the world
on this your birthday.
Great decisions have been
made—
perhaps things done today
will go down in history—
but hardly anyone knows
what I've been doing:
giving you, my child,
a happy birthday.

Yet I have made
something durable,
something that cannot
be touched by time,
something no one
can take away from you.
With the help of God,
and with my love, I have
made happy memories,
something money on its own
can never buy.

Is it a waste of time caring
about little things?
No, for in eternity
they are most important
and most precious.
I am glad that I can
make joyful memories
for you. Yes, I am content
to spend my time
giving you a happy childhood.

Shells
FROM A CONVERSATION
WITH MY SON

Copper, orange,
pink, white,
brown, black,
blue, green,
gray, stripy,
shimmering, silvery—

I like
the color of shells.

Rough, lumpy,
smooth, shiny,
sharp, hard,
broken, fragile,
zigzag round the edges—

I like
the feel of shells.

Big, small,
long, thin,
tiny, spiral,

half-circles, fans,
shallow cups,
little rowing boats,
cone-shaped hats—

I like
the shape of shells.

Some joined in pairs,
some on their own,
still sandy
and smelling of the sea,
they are really amazing,
marvelous,
brilliant—

I wonder
who lived in this shell?

A mother's meditation on Christmas Eve

I can't put my children's presents by their beds, for they still aren't asleep. So I thought I'd spend some time sitting quietly while I'm waiting. I sometimes think that no one can possibly know how busy parents are at Christmas and how much work and planning go into just one day of celebration. Is it all worth it?

If all my preparations are done out of love then they can lead my children to the God of love. If they are done out of duty or even resentment then the true meaning of Christmas is lost. All the trimmings become an end in themselves, like a beautifully wrapped-up box with nothing in it. Let me always prepare Christmas for them with love and remember that time is short to give children happy memories.

They have gone to sleep at last! I've put their presents, all knobbly and interesting, at the ends of their beds. I'm exhausted! I don't know how I'm going to keep awake tomorrow. But perhaps that in itself is a reminder of Christmas: it's more important to give than it is to receive. And perhaps, in the giving, in some way I cannot see, I may find God after all.

The touch of love

Like evening shadows
lengthening from the west,
my prayers stretch
over our child
and beyond to the unborn,
our children's children,
to all generations
that shall spring from us
until the end of time.

I pray that they may be loved
with the love
that comes from Jesus
and so love others
in their turn,
handing it on
like a blazing torch,
a gift for every
generation.

So that from my prayers
may spring an endless
chain of light
stretching into eternity.
And so no child of ours
will be untouched by love
and not one go unblessed.

I pray that you may have your roots and foundation in love.

EPHESIANS 3:17

May the Lord bless you and take care of you;
may the Lord be kind and gracious to you;
may the Lord look on you with favor and give you
peace.

NUMBERS 6:24–26

Shared joy

You are yourself, my child,
not a replica of me
nor of anyone.
You will have your own ideas
of what is beautiful.

So moments of shared joy,
when gladness glows
in both of us
because some fragment of glory
has touched our lives
at the same time,
are rare and precious—
not to be grasped at,
not to be expected,
or accepted as our right,
but to be treasured
as an unmerited gift of God.

Your children are not your children.
They are sons and daughters of Life's longing for itself.
They come through you but not from you,
And though they are with you yet they belong not to you.

You may give them your love but not your thoughts,
For they have their own thoughts.
You may house their bodies but not their souls,
For their souls dwell in the house of tomorrow,
which you cannot visit, not even in your dreams.

KAHLIL GIBRAN

Snowflakes

I stood and watched the snow falling on a winter's afternoon. The sky was full of swirling white flakes blown by the wind into wild and intricate dances. When the sun rose the next morning the whole world was blanketed in white and the snow was several inches deep.

I wondered how many billions of snowflakes it must have taken just to cover the road outside my house. I read once that if you look at snowflakes through a microscope you will discover that no two flakes have been of the same design and, as far as they can tell, this has been so since the beginning of time.

There are far fewer people in the world than there are snowflakes! If God takes such care designing individual snowflakes, how much more must he care about each human being, to make everyone unique and different.

Out of the shadows

Every day, it seems, I hear of children dying of hunger, being orphaned by war, being abused, or deliberately exposed to all kinds of evil. And tonight, as I looked at my own child, over whose sleeping head so many prayers have been whispered, I thought of all the children in the world who have no one to pray for them.

So, Lord, I pray for these children, bringing them out of the shadows of the world into your presence, so that they will not pass through darkness untouched by light. I hardly know how to begin to pray for them. Touch them, all those who dwell in darkness, with light, love and joy. And though I weep because my heart is not large enough to shelter them all, I know that there is room for every one of them to dwell in your heart for ever.

Privileged mother

Tonight a cold wind howls outside. The windows are shut, the curtains are drawn and my children are asleep under warm bedclothes. Tomorrow morning they will have a hot breakfast and go to school well clad against the cold. During the day their clothes will be washed in heated water and in the afternoon they will come back to a comfortable home and a hot meal.

Lord, accept my thanks for every one of these luxuries. Thank you that I have never had to say to them, 'I have no clothes or blankets to keep you warm.' Thank you that I have never had to see them cry with cold.

I know I am a very privileged mother. Help me always to be grateful and to remember all the mothers in the world who are not as blessed as I am. Thank you, Lord, that on this and every night I can keep my children warm.

The embroidery prayer

Lord, if one day my eyes grow dim
and my fingers too unsteady
to stitch embroidery
as I am doing now,
grant to me that I may not
grow bitter at my failing powers
but that I may be able
to re-channel the creative skills
that you have given me.

So that, although I can no longer
make beauty with thread and fabric,
I may be able to embroider
your beauty into other people's lives
—with my prayers.

The patient making
of beautiful things
has much
to commend it
and is an echo
of heaven.

Knitting

It's lovely to see you
wearing clothes
I have knitted for you.
some were made before
you were born.
The glowing colors
suit you so well.

Yes, I love
knitting for you.
Strands of hope,
longing and tenderness
are mingled with the wool.
And so I see you,
not just warmly dressed,
but clothed with love.

G ROWING UP

Ten years old

What does it mean
to be ten years old?

Muddy jacket,
untied shoelaces,
torn trousers,
grubby fingernails,
no handkerchief.

Bulging pockets,
endless collections,
successive hobbies,
perpetual questions,
amazing discoveries.

Tripping over,
crashing into,
losing possessions,
thinking big,
starving hungry.

Exasperating,
endearing,
demanding,
exhausting,
rewarding—
and *alive!*

That's what it means
to be ten years old!

Finding your own way

Who are you, my child?
I know you
and yet I do not know you.

Now I can look down at you
but soon you will be taller than me.
You live in my world
and yet belong to your own world.

And sometimes, in brief moments
between our times of busyness,
we stop for long enough
to look into each other's eyes.

And I remember
that being your mom
is not all cooking, cleaning,
nagging and clearing up.

You tug at your moorings
yet you know you need a harbor.
You need time and space
To find your own country.

And though I lead you there
I am the one who must
wait outside while you
go in and possess it.
And even then
I can only enter at your invitation.

In these brief, shared moments
I see it in your eyes—
that you have begun to find
your own country—
and I am very glad for you, my child,
yes, I am very glad.

If a child lives with criticism
He learns to condemn.

If a child lives with hostility
He learns to fight.

If a child lives with ridicule
He learns to be shy.

If a child lives with shame
He learns to feel guilty.

If a child lives with tolerance
He learns to be patient.

If a child lives with encouragement
He learns confidence.

If a child lives with praise
He learns to appreciate.

If a child lives with fairness
He learns justice.

If a child lives with security
He learns to have faith.

If a child lives with approval
He learns to like himself.

If a child lives with acceptance and
friendship
He learns to find love in the world.

DOROTHY LAW NOLTE

When they leave home

I have seen
so many parents
grow bitter when
their children leave home,
as if they were all
they had to live for;
as if they had let
their children imprison them
instead of letting
them go free.

Lord, in your mercy,
do not let this happen to me.
Let my children help me
to be a more loving person
and when they have left,
may I not feel cast off,
rejected or bitter
because they no longer
need me in the same way.
Help me to accept that I cannot
always love them in the ways
that I would choose.
But let me be willing to give
that love to anyone around me
who needs to be loved.

Made in God's image

God made me as a person in my own right, and while I am happy to spend a large amount of my time looking after other people, he understands my need to be apart and to build up my own identity. I must have time to myself, outside and inside the home, and the opportunity to discover and develop my own gifts. For this will enrich my family relationships and enable me to come back to them with my love refreshed and renewed.

God made me and I belong to him, so I am not just somebody's wife or somebody's mother but someone of importance, someone precious, for I am a woman in my own right. I am a child of God and he made me in his own image.

Whoever glorifies his mother is like one who
lays up treasure.

SIRACH 1:1–2

When your mother is old show her your
appreciation.

PROVERBS 23:22

Respect your father and mother, so that you
may live a long time in the land that I am
giving you.

EXODUS 20:12